GW00470242

Unschooling as Homeschooling

Unschooling as Homeschooling

A Beginners Guide for Getting Started

Written by
Starr Green

Earthy Info
Corvallis, Oregon

Copyright © 2021 by Starr Green

All rights reserved. No part of this book may
be reproduced or used in any manner without
written permission of the copyright owner except
for the use of quotations in a book review. For
more information, email: hello@earthyinfo.com.

First edition September 2021

Illustrations by: Megan Scott
Cover design by: Earthy Info
Interior book design by: Earthy Info

ISBN 978-1-955561-10-5 (softcover)
ISBN 978-1-955561-11-2 (ebook)

Library of Congress Control Number: 2021945612

Earthy Info
Corvallis, Oregon
www.earthyinfo.com

"The noblest pleasure is the joy of understanding."

-Leonardo da Vinci

This book's formatting adds it to the growing list of titles intentionally designed using The British Dyslexia Association's style guide for easier reading. Adjustments include a carefully selected font on cream paper, more space between the letters, more space between the lines of text, and a jagged right edge. Also, providing a smoother reading experience with shorter sentences, paragraphs, and chapters. To learn more, visit the publisher's website.

Table of Contents

CHAPTER 1
Successful Lives

One day in late spring, at seven years old, I walked six blocks home from second grade in scorching hundred-degree Arizona heat. From my elementary school classroom, past the middle school, across a bustling intersection, around a bizarrely eye-watering-pink painted apartment complex, to warily creep past the dilapidated halfway house, and finally a blocks-long stretch home through a run-down neighborhood of ranch houses built in the fifties, to finally arrive at the corner house we rented. A sprawling single-story four-bedroom, oddly shaped and covered in tan stucco, surrounded by a dust bowl of powdery topsoil instead of grass. An eyesore all the neighbors hated looking at. Skipping inside through the never-locked kitchen door, I was shocked to see my mother waiting for me at the dining room table. She was smiling.

Unnerved, I dropped my backpack and edged toward her. Artificially cheery, mom launched to a clearly prepared pitch on the joys of homeschooling. I relaxed a bit. She described a utopia of learning. Picking my own topics, learning at my own pace, avoiding early mornings, cruel peers, and despicable school lunches. In the end, she asked if I wanted to homeschool, and I accepted.

Despite a promising start, the utopia ended fairly quickly. By day three, mom decided her actual presence in the room was not needed, as I learned. Handing me an empty planning grid, with subjects on one side and days of the week along the top, she explained how to plan lessons. Then left me to it.

For the first three years, a new stack of textbooks was ordered in my grade level, and I'd do my best to work my way through them. I took the confusing bits to mom for a while, who breezily sent me to ask dad. So, I'd show dad, who looked closely at the whole chapter only to shrug helplessly with an apologetic smile. I learned to skip the confusing parts until I eventually skipped all of them to focus on reading library books. Soon, my mom stopped ordering textbooks. For both my brother and me.

Later, I discovered my family's switch to homeschooling had nothing to do with me directly. Mother was sick of the school system. She said it gave her children a bad attitude. So, prompted by the rantings of a disgruntled elementary school principal, she pulled all her children out the same year.

My brother, about to start kindergarten before we quit school, never attended public school. While he was five and six, I taught him to read, write, and basic math using worksheets. For reasons I still don't know, my mom told me to stop, and he was left on his own for learning. He and I played card games, board games, and silly childhood games. I often read aloud to him because he didn't enjoy reading, but loved to hear the stories. So, he grew up with no traditional schooling at all.

I knew my upbringing had been unconventional, so I never intended to homeschool my kids. My mom was odd. Normal parents sent their kids to school. Right?

However, my oldest daughter never fit into the system well. She resisted learning to read. The teacher's condescending attitude grated on her tiny nerves. As a high-strung redhead, her temper often overwhelmed sense, so she was a target for bullies because they could get an easy rise out of her. By the time she hit middle school, she was disillusioned with the whole elementary school system, and middle school was even worse. Now there were more teachers, more kids, and worse, a confusing schedule in various classrooms.

A month in, my eleven-year-old was depressed, having almost daily panic attacks, and refusing to get on the bus in the morning. I started taking her to school and forcing her to go inside. Several months in, she was in therapy, friendless, and telling me her life felt hopeless. Not what you want to hear from a young child. If a school makes you need therapy to get through it, maybe it's not worth your energy to keep trying to make it work?

We clearly needed a big life change. Considering pulling her out of school, I looked into various homeschooling curriculum. As I did, I came across unschooling. It struck me that both my brother and I were basically unschooled. We spent each day doing what came naturally, researching what interested us or reading all day. Playing and learning at the same time. When it came time to buckle down for college, we both had to do a couple of remedial math courses, but they were the only consequence of our unconventional unschooling upbringing.

My brother stopped at age 7, I stopped at age 10, and my daughter at age 11. For various reasons, none of us continued with traditionally assigned schoolwork. What did we do with our time? How did we all turn out?

I plowed through a book a day, reading much of the juvenile nonfiction section. Eventually finishing my library's entire young adult section. Now I'm a writer and book publisher with a degree in Communications.

My brother spent time out in the neighborhood chatting with people instead of doing any lessons at all and only listening to audiobooks. Now he's a bilingual translator with a degree in Linguistics.

My daughter spent days or weeks on digital art projects while watching nonfiction videos about drawing better. Now she's a freelance illustrator.

Choosing your own learning path is important in wanting to learn.

I'm autistic and grew up in the 90s. My autistic brother is a social butterfly who grew up in the 2000s. My daughter has ADHD and dyslexia and grew up in the 2010s.

These three very different situations show the era or personality don't matter. If you do a lot of what you love, you'll get better at it and understand it more. You'll be successful at it. Many examples exist throughout history.

Thomas Edison was taught math and reading by his mother, then was left alone to work on his inventions as much as he wanted.

Louis Armstrong had a rough life. He was raised by several different people and quit school at eleven years old. He sang with other boys in the streets for money and eventually learned to play the trumpet through his teen years. Captivating music is what he is still known for.

Kept home from school, Agatha Christie loved reading and was writing her own works by age 10. A hundred years later, her books — and the movies and tv show made from them — have their own subcategory in murder mysteries.

One biographer complained that inconsistent homeschooling due to constant trips around the world caused gaps of knowledge for Teddy Roosevelt. Although, it could be argued all the animals and natural places he was allowed to explore during his extravagant upbringing allowed a lifelong interest in nature. Leading to historic moments in his presidency when, despite opposition from Congress, Teddy Roosevelt created the first wild bird preserves, founded the United States Forest Service, and established five national parks.

CHAPTER 2

What is Unschooling?

Traditional school is a twelve-year commitment. Enforced by parents because school is the social norm. Although, for a moment, imagine any twelve years of your life. Long time, right? Can you imagine committing to any project every day for twelve long years? Especially one you didn't pick? Honestly, the thought is horrifying.

Now imagine those same twelve years were given to you as a gift. You don't have to work. You could do absolutely anything you want at any moment of the day. What projects could you finish? What could you accomplish? The possibilities are endless!

More importantly, what would your emotional mindset be at the end of these two different twelve-year experiments?

The current school system is based on the idea we must force children to learn because if left alone, they would never do schoolwork assignments on their own. That's true. Children would never assign themselves an essay or a spelling test, so they must be forced to do those things. However, the concept has one flaw. Worksheets and assignments are not the only way to learn. Schoolwork is in place to teach a large group of people one subject quickly.

Traditional schooling is learning in a classroom with a teacher. Homeschooling is learning the same information, but at home with a tutor or parent as a teacher. While unschooling is a bit more wild and freeform. Unschooling is a version of homeschooling. So, if anyone asks, you can simply say your kids are homeschooled. Homeschooling is a big umbrella term and unschooling falls under it. In practice, though, the two have big differences in approach.

While it's true we must force children to do schoolwork assignments, we don't need to force them to learn. Learning comes naturally to humans. Back to our twelve-year experiment, no matter what odd thing you choose to do for twelve years, you would be learning something. You would not be able to help it.

As an adult example of unschooling, take British rectors and vicars over the last few hundred years. They were paid a salary to tend local parishes, the church communities of a single town. They took care of the church building, assisted in town committees, and gave a sermon on Sunday. It gives a person quite a lot of free time. Usually the younger sons of gentry landowners, these men were a social class above the townsfolk and not accustomed to hard labor. So, they spent their days in intellectual pursuits.

With the chance to spend endless time on their hobbies, collectively, these bored men and their children became writers, inventors, scientists, musicians, gardeners, and astronomers. Gaining fame as master experts on everything from plant diseases to spiders to loom weaving to dog breeding. One genius math fan invented Bayes theorem in the mid-1700s. A calculation so before it's time it can only be solved with a computer.

With enough free time on your hands, what hobby would you pursue? What could your children learn with endless hours of "free time" to focus on what they find interesting?

There have been so many successful vicars it's hard to see past the astonishing numbers. However, many vicars chose not to find pursuits outside the church. Instead, they spent time visiting the community. Or simply frittered away the spare hours. If you take an average classroom, you will see the same divisions. Perhaps 80% of the kids want to learn. Another 15% only want to socialize. The last 5% are not interested in participating at all.

Many of the kids that want to learn are being stunted by a test-driven school system. Those kids who want to socialize would learn more from talking to each other and collaborating. Those kids not participating are not learning anything in the classroom anyway, so they might as well be at home learning by living life.

I readily admit I might have a skewed view of rote learning. Neurodiversity might play a part in why everyone I know has not done well in school, including me and my brother and my own kids. Also, any friends I make are neurodiverse, as are their children who are not happy in school. It's possible some kids thrive in a school environment, but I've yet to meet one in person.

So, by not visiting a school building for the bulk of every day or doing homework through the weekends, does it mean your child will stop having classes, lessons, or learning?

The short answer is no. It doesn't mean they will never take a formal lesson or do another worksheet. An unschooling lifestyle change means they get to pick their own learning. Maybe they'll choose online nutrition courses. Or a guitar lesson at a local music store. Or watch endless videos about space.

After getting settled into unschooling, at about a year in, an average week for my ADHD 12-year-old daughter was a lot of sketching, a tiny bit of ukulele, daily practice in Japanese on Duolingo, videos about astronomy and Japan. Along with chores, making her own lunch, and playing video games.

Meanwhile, an average week for my autistic 9-year-old, along with the same chores and meal prep, was reading some fiction, writing short stories, and a little piano practice. However, the bulk of her time was spent playing Minecraft or watching hours of videos about Minecraft. Mostly all she did for two years after leaving school and it seemed such a pointless waste of time. Yet, I held my tongue, and now she designs her own modifications to the game and has picked out a college based on its computer programming degree.

Everything learned as an adult is considered life experience, and everything learned in school is school experience, but what if life experience could start a lot sooner? Commit to child-led learning. Trust and respect your children's choices, and who knows where it could lead.

The week we pulled my oldest out of school, her class was working its way through a unit about war. She was stressing out over her writing assignment. An essay on The History of Helmets. Not only does she not care about helmets at all, but she's also not a big fan of history.

Imagine government-forced learning had continued as adults. As part of your 35-year-old curriculum you must learn the names of lake shapes. You know you will never ever need to use these names, but you are handed a list with graphics of the shapes and told you must memorize them in under a week for a test. Even if you ace the test, shapes of lakes is something you never asked to learn and will never use again. In ten years, the chances of you remembering lake shape names are low.

However, let's say you decide to take up quilting. You read about it, watch some videos, maybe learn from a local or join a group. You purchase a bunch of supplies and spend hours practicing. You make a dozen quilts before something else catches your eye. In ten years, the chances of you remembering how to quilt are high because you cared about it and spent time becoming proficient.

Mastering something tricky when you want to learn it is satisfying. Learning something hard when you don't want to is stressful. The overriding message of school is that learning is difficult. When people believe doing something will be difficult, they naturally don't want to do it. The more they are coerced, the greater the resistance.

Yet, we take naturally curious toddlers, sit them down in kindergarten, and start drilling them on numbers and letters. Putting on a lot of pressure to learn and learn quickly to keep up with their classmates. Setting levels of knowledge to achieve, and increasing the difficulty each year, sets the wrong tone for joyful learning.

I once met an 11-year-old girl obsessed with school. We were tossed together one night because we were close in age, and the whole time she made us "play school." She was the teacher, and I was the student. She sat me at the desk in her room and assigned things for me to do. "Write 2+2 on a paper and solve it. Then I'll grade it," she said. It was the dullest game I'd ever played.

Unschooling is the opposite of that game, but more importantly, it's the opposite of "school." No assignments from lessons. No curriculum. Never any quizzes or testing. No grading or teachers. No textbooks or classic school supplies. No massive amounts of time required for lesson planning. Simply learning for the joy of learning.

The best part of unschooling as homeschooling, is the parent stays a parent instead of a teacher. Even better, the child gets to remain a child instead of a student.

The main thing is to let children focus on what they love best, and the rest of the subjects will end up touched on through that main interest. So, trust your child will learn what is meaningful to them. More importantly, their learning will stick because they care about it. It's important to let go. Leave behind your ideas about what learning "should be" and move forward with what learning can be.

CHAPTER 3

How to Use This Book

○────────────○────────────○

Child-led learning is not, I repeat not, sitting around doing nothing until your child has an idea. Instead, it's offering them multiple paths and respecting their choice when they make one. You could offer math learning videos, Spanish language practice, or library book reading. From those, they could pick reading for the rest of the day.

Or, from those offered options, they could pick none of them and choose to message with a friend instead. At first glance, a disappointing turn of events. However, they would still be learning. In chatting online with friends, kids are both reading and writing while practicing social skills — all at the same time! Which is much better than simply reading one book.

Even better if they are playing a game while chatting with their friends. I've watched my girls play several online games with typed communication to old and new friends. Roblox and Jumpstart are two that come to mind with chat boxes and learning games. What an outsider might perceive as letting your child play games for hours is instead teaching them quite a lot. Hand-eye coordination, social skills, reading, writing, rule-following, multi-tasking, and also whatever the actual game is trying to teach, such as spelling or subtraction.

When playing Minecraft, my daughters looked up all kinds of information. Interest-based research has improved their reading levels and comprehension. Further, my eldest chose to learn the complex multiplication required to make her Minecraft building structurally sound. Next, she learned a bunch about architecture to make it pretty. If I had sat her down and tried to have her memorize the same multiplication, she would have been too bored to concentrate. Yet, my kid studied these things on her own because she found a real-world problem to apply them to.

My daughter had a good point. She asked, "What do you think would happen if they didn't have classes at my Middle School? If they opened up all the doors and told the students to go anywhere in the school they wanted. They could talk to friends on the cafeteria benches. Play instruments in the music room. Do science experiments in the lab. Or anything they wanted. Do you think they'd still learn?"

My answer? YES. In fact, that sounds like the best possible way to do school. Have a teacher in each room to guide learning, but let kids wander in and out, or spend all day in the place they find most interesting. Will they have what educators call "gaps" in their knowledge. For sure. Do they have "gaps" in their knowledge with the current education system? Absolutely.

By memorizing information from textbooks and taking tests to prove knowledge, the quickly learned and quickly lost data is a pointless waste of time in the long run. It creates as many gaps in knowledge as not stressing over uninteresting topics in the first place.

Textbook companies disagree. They are always about to create the next perfect curriculum. However, there is no perfect curriculum to teach every child. It doesn't exist. Schools try to teach the bulk of the students what the state decides are the most important topics to prepare them for an eventual college education. The kids that don't fit into the system are given extra mini-group classes to "get them up to grade level," stressing them further.

No contrived learning is retained in a meaningful way. It's not long-term learning because forced learning is not how humans gain understanding.

This is where unschooling comes in. I wish it had a better non-school-related name. Perhaps Life Learning or Enthusiastic Learning. Whatever you call it, it is the perfect curriculum because it's custom-built for each child by that child. I mentioned in Chapter 1, we don't know what types of things will be most important to learn for any child's future. So, if they are allowed to let their interests guide them, they will instinctively learn what they need to know.

Every day of every minute, humans learn. We can't help it. Humans, none of us, exist in a vacuum. We are learning. Constantly. As adults, we consume news, podcasts, nonfiction and fiction books, documentaries, movies, and TV shows. Even in gossiping with coworkers, you learn new juicy info while social bonding. In short, humans never ever stop learning. We don't do it formally like in school, by being handed a book on trigonometry or told to start playing the recorder.

The beautiful thing is, we could learn trigonometry and the recorder if we suddenly wanted to, but no one is forcing an adult to do those things.

Imagine you have some time to binge-watch a TV show. You might spend a long time browsing, sampling a few shows, and deciding you are not interested in them. Finally, you click on a promising one, and about 15 minutes in, you know this is a good show. A show you are going to enjoy. You can just feel it. Think about that feeling of giddy discovery. Whether the show's details are something you need to know or not, you're about to spend the next 10 or more hours learning about its world and its characters. How exciting!

The following chapters have topics with

selections of subtopics you can present to your children. You are the content provider, and this book is a browsing menu. So, a few times a week, ask your kids to spend at least 15 minutes on a new subtopic. If they get interested, awesome! If they don't, simply move on to the next subtopic or resource later. When you are not presenting new ideas, the kids can do or learn whatever they are most interested in — with or without your participation.

After unschooling for a couple of years, you will no longer need this tasting menu of options. Parents can still occasionally present ideas kids might enjoy, but by living in a way comfortable to them, kids will naturally find interesting stuff on their own. Your child will have settled into child-led learning and no longer separate "learning time" and "playing time." The goal, eventually, is to transition to a world without subjects and instead simply live life.

In the meantime, I hope the topics in this book will smooth the transition. I've gathered the most common learning themes, organized them under recognizable school subjects, then explained each a little deeper in the context of unschooling. Instead of spending time researching subtopic options to provide for your children, it's all right here at your fingertips.

CHAPTER 4
Art & Music

Art

--Learning Options: learning videos, making art, reading books about historical art, taking classes

--Topics: Animation, Ceramics, Charcoal, Digital Drawing, Drawing, Felting, Film (making videos), Floral Design, Food(culinary art), Literature (writing), Painting, Performing (acting), Photography, Sculpture, Sewing, Watercolor

I've put art first because it's one of the things humans love most. We're excited about cave drawings, we revere past societies that revered art, and it's really fun to do.

When thinking of art, many people think of paint and canvas, or framed paintings in a museum. However, art has created many of the things in your home. Your plates are a form of art, the TV shows you watch are art, your furniture was designed.

Currently, education is veering toward STEM curriculum. Science, Technology, Engineering, and Math. They seem to have forgotten that humans need art. Building a bridge is important, but building a beautiful bridge is iconic.

It's easy to encourage your children in art. Everything from computer animation and digital drawing to garden design and ceramics. Pursuing art is a great time to offer your kids classes. Our local bakery offers cake-making classes for kids, which would be considered culinary art. Or, we have a local musical theater kids club for the performing arts.

Giving your child a taste of all the different art in the world, not only the framed kind, might inspire them in unpredictable ways.

Music

--Learning Options: learning videos, taking classes, practicing what you've learned

--Topics: learning an instrument (guitar, piano, ukulele, violin), music history, playing music, writing music

If your kids are interested in music, they could do voice lessons or instrument lessons from a variety of instruments to choose from. The classic piano and guitar lessons, or instruments from other countries. Also, if your child wants to join a band, there are usually programs for homeschooled children to join electives at their local high school, so definitely look into that.

Beyond instruments, other music options include writing music the old-fashioned way, creating digital music, or making videos. If they've already learned an instrument, they can do performances or make videos of themselves playing. With the ability to post videos online, many people find their niche in creating content for the whole world to watch.

CHAPTER 5
History & Languages

History

--Learning Options: Learning videos, reading books, taking classes

--Topics: American History, Famous People, Rights Movements, Wars, and Conflicts ~ History by ▪ Continent, Country, Region, Era/Age, Period ~ History of ▪ Art, Culture, Religion, Science, Technology

When I was nine, I discovered the biography section in the juvenile nonfiction area of my library. I read about Queen Elizabeth the Pirate Queen, and I was hooked. I started at the letter A and methodically worked my way through the whole section. Many children want to learn about the past.

If your child is only interested in history, no worries. There is so much history to learn that some people specialize their whole career in one type of history. War buffs, celebrity experts, and science history nerds.

With so many to choose from, present your child with chances to learn about lots of cultures and countries. With too many to even list, I've left category ideas in this topic to explore. Some suggestions are: Egyptian Civilizations, Greek Legends, Black American History, Japanese Culture. It doesn't have to be in a book either. We've attended a Scandinavian Summer Beltane, visited a Native American museum, Blues Festival, Danish Tulip Farm, and more. History can be fascinating!

Social Studies

--Learning Options: learning videos, reading books, taking classes

--Topics: Anthropology, Archaeology, Current Events and News, Economics, Geography, Global News, History, Human Behavior, Laws, Legends and Mythology, Philosophy, Political Science, Psychology, Religion, Sociology

Social studies is a bit like history, but it's more about the history of people or issues with people. Think current events in the news, even global news, or economics and politics. Some psychology and philosophy can fit in here. My daughter finds philosophy especially interesting.

Also, fitting in here is a lot about past cultures. Not just the history of past cultures, which sort of fit into the history category above, but more about human behavior. What were their laws and legends in those past cultures? Anthropology and archaeology both land in the section because they are more about people than simply history.

Languages

--*Learning Options: learning apps, learning videos, classes, practice with a partner*

--*Topics: French, Gaelic, German, Italian, Japanese, Sign Language, Spanish*

Language also goes in this chapter because it fits into history and social studies, culture studies, and past and current languages. Planning a trip to a different country is a lot more fun when you study a bit first to know some of the language.

CHAPTER 6

Reading & Writing

Reading Fiction

--Learning Options: physical books, audiobooks, online fiction blogs, fan fiction

--Topics: Adventure, Fantasy, Graphic Novels, Mystery, Romance, SciFi

Reading is my very favorite. As a teen, I was constantly reading. If I'd finished a book or was in a boring place, I read anything in front of me. Cereal boxes, street signs, toothpaste tubes, anything. When I tore through my stack of library books too quickly and had nothing else to read, I pulled out the encyclopedia set. What I needed was the internet, where it's impossible to run out of things to read.

I was sure my kids would embrace reading too. It started well. For their birthday my girls are allowed to choose anywhere in the city they want to go. My three-year-old chose the library. I have a picture of her hugging her favorite book in the children's section. However, I hadn't planned on how frustrated the kids would become with reading after going to school.

By the time they started unschooling it was too late. They felt books were something to be avoided. They had been tortured with these devices for far too long and would not willingly use one. No matter how many amazing books I requested from the library on their behalf, I could rarely get them to actually crack any of the books open. Even now, even at higher reading levels, they still don't choose to read for fun. It's disheartening.

I've tried several ways to encourage reading with my girls. Options that worked included: flat out bribery, providing books with tv show characters they already liked, and putting in a little extra effort on my part to search for graphic novels in their reading levels.

I've also had quite a bit of luck offering to read to them. Very similar to my brother, reading was hard, so listening was preferable.

I don't have any astonishing words of wisdom here on how to force your kids to read, other than to say you shouldn't. It's something they want to do or isn't. If reading books stresses them out, find a way to make it easier until they are literate. Then consider letting it go for a while. They may never enjoy reading (sadly), but luckily savoring books is not a requirement of adulthood.

Reading Nonfiction

--Learning Options: reliable website, physical book, magazine, audiobook

--Topics: See all topics in History, Science, Social Studies

Nonfiction is similar. If the kids don't want to read, they won't easily learn by reading. Books are the main way I learn things. When I get obsessed with a new topic, I run to the library and get about six books on it. My girls are from a different generation and grew up with different tools. When they want to learn something, they look up a video about it.

I've decided the path doesn't matter. As long as we all end up learning something, it doesn't matter if I learned it through a book and they learned it through video. Although, it doesn't mean I can't live in hope. So, similar to fiction books, I often requested selections from the library I thought might tempt them. I'd leave these offerings on their bed, on the couch, or around the house. Especially during the first years of unschooling.

My girls mostly didn't bother with the nonfiction library books scattered around our home. Although, when they want to know something and they can't find a video, they will read a website about it, and that's what matters. Moving past books, many places online post nonfiction. So, I taught my children the difference between reputable and sketchy sites, then left them to their research.

Writing

--Learning Options: writing about a topic, writing a book review, creating a fiction story, building a slide show around a single topic, or typing practice

--Topics: See all topics in History, Science, Social Studies

Writing often gets lumped in with reading, but it's a very different thing. It's much the difference between watching a TV show and directing a TV show. The level of involvement is vastly different. Not everyone is going to be good at writing or enjoy it.

My oldest likes storytelling, but not actually writing, so she does her storytelling through digital art. My youngest chose to write a few fiction short stories but has moved past that and not returned to it. At her age, I also wrote short fiction stories, but through my teen years only wrote book reviews for the library's teen newsletter as a volunteer. I didn't start creative writing again until I was an adult.

If you think of writing as an art or an elective, you realize not everyone needs to produce long writing assignments. Creative writing is like algebra. It's not usually needed in day-to-day life.

So, I've taught my girls basic life skills writing. Emails, messages, lists, meal plans, and more. Made sure they can use Google Docs if they need to write something more substantial in the future. Then I left it alone and metaphorically walked away.

My best advice is to explain why something is needed, and that will help them become motivated enough to learn the bits of writing that will be important for their future.

CHAPTER 7
Math & Science

Math

--Learning Options: Khan Academy and other learning Websites

--Topics: learn by grade level or what is interesting

Honestly, if your kids never choose math, it's 100% fine. I know there's a big push for math at schools these days. However, when was the last time you needed to know the different names of triangles?

My oldest daughter stopped learning math in sixth grade, my youngest in fourth grade. I also stopped learning math in fourth grade and my brother stopped learning math in first grade. When I say I stopped learning math, I mean formally, but we still learned through living life.

Math comes up through life on occasion. When working out percentages of a sales price or figuring out travel time during a vacation. For all of those times, you have the internet and a calculator. None of them require algebra or even pre-algebra.

Later on, when homeschooled children take the GED to graduate, they will need to know some geometry and pre-algebra. The online classes the kids will take right before the GED teaches them everything they need to know to pass. Then they can move on to college. From my experience, math is easier to learn when you're older and you have a specific reason to study it.

After my brother finished his GED, he started at community college with a remedial course on basic math and another on pre-algebra and the third about algebra. I did the same. This is a much quicker and more logical way to learn math than spread over the years in pieces.

As an adult, I took all the math basics in a row in a single year, starting with pre-algebra. This approach provided the building blocks I needed to understand the classes for my science degree. Courses in College Algebra, Probabilities, Statics, math-based Chemistry classes, and Micro Biology classes with a lot of math in them.

In contrast, my friend tried to go to college and took a placement test for math. He remembered just enough of the concepts he learned in high school to place into college math. There he proceeded to fail a math class and a math-based chemistry class. He simply didn't remember enough of the math he was taught growing up to succeed with it years down the road. He refused to take the remedial math courses to retake the math classes he failed. So, he never went back to college and decades later still has no career.

Stuffing kids' heads with math before they are ready for it, and if they're not interested in learning it, is a pointless waste of their time. We have used math workbooks for my girls when they needed to prepare for a state test or the GED. So, unschooling doesn't mean never learning math. It's simply the freedom to choose to learn it when they are ready, in the mood, or when it's necessary for their future. At that point, they will be motivated to learn and it will stick better.

Science

--Learning Options: learning videos, reading books, taking classes

--Topics: Anatomy, Astronomy, Biology, Botany, Chemistry, Climatology, Earth Science, Environmental Studies, First Aid, Geology, Health Studies, Nutrition, Oceanography, Physics, Science History, Zoology

So much to cover with science! It's a big umbrella holding a lot of varied topics. Everything from the elements that create water to first-aid to what's at the bottom of a volcano. I've only listed a few ways to learn science here, including videos, books, and classes. Although science kits are a lot of fun too. You can buy one individually, or find ones on a monthly subscription, so you can do a science experiment per month. I've signed my daughter up for those before and she likes them a lot.

The science topics above have almost endless sub subtopics, so I didn't even attempt to list them all out. For example, if your child's interested in Botany, they can narrow it down to plant genetics, history of trees, plant identification, strain breeding, ornamental gardening, vegetable gardening, and more.

For a while, my youngest was obsessed with the ocean, while my oldest was obsessed with anatomy. Those both shifted to computer science and nutrition, respectively.

Humans are naturally curious and love to learn about the world around us. Science is one of the easiest sells when presenting new topics to kids. Most of the time, they'll go out and find information themselves, but you are welcome to present interesting topics as you come across them.

CHAPTER 8
Social & Playing

Social

--Time with: Pet, Friend, Sister, Dad, Mom, Aunt, Uncle, Grandma, or online game friends

Learning through life is the basis of unschooling. So, it seems slightly odd to have its own chapter. Yet, I couldn't leave these important bits out. Your child may turn down all the subjects you offer. They won't be interested in history, flat out refuse to read, only have a passing interest in anything science-related, and not be musically talented. Honestly, that's okay.

They can still live life in a way that makes them happy. If they need to learn later for college or for a job, they are just as capable of learning at a later time, probably more so. In the meantime, they might be interested in communicating or playing. Also, they should still be helping out around the house to learn life skills. That's what this chapter is about.

I set up my children's messenger service with contacts for extended family. I encouraged them to message their grandparents, aunts, uncles, and friends. What was a fun activity for my social butterfly, was a disastrous turn of events for my autistic, socially challenged daughter. I didn't force either of them to participate, but I made it available, and consequently, they messaged family members more than they would have if messaging wasn't an option.

Playing

--Card Games, Board Games, Video Games, Movies, Shows, Online Videos, Puzzles

It's key to remember how important play is because humans often learn best through play. Video games are no exception. I've seen my daughter play a game and chat with people for hours. As I mentioned above in one of the first few chapters, she is learning an amazing amount of skills while doing something that looks easy and pointless. She is learning to both long-term focus and to multi-task. She's reading and writing in the chatbox with friends. She is learning rule-following, hand-eye coordination, and puzzle-solving.

On top of that, many of the games she picks are learning games. They have their own agenda for teaching things like typing, spelling, or math. Even if they're playing Minecraft instead of a learning game, there's quite a bit of creativity, art, math, and architectural savvy involved in creating many of the things they build.

Away from computer games, card games and board games also provide a challenging puzzle for the mind. Regular everyday play through life is a great way to learn.

Tidying

--Tidy Bedroom, Dishes, Counters, Front Room/ Entry, Bathroom, Laundry, Vacuum, Sweep, Pets

I started teaching my oldest daughter to clean at around 15 months old. She was barely walking steadily. When she dropped a banana peel, instead of picking it up myself, I had her pick it up and walked her to the trash to throw it away. She's been learning to take care of herself ever since.

The basic elements of caring for yourself are surprisingly hard to learn. The important thing to note is knowing how to care for yourself is a big confidence boost. So, without it being too stressful if possible, start your kids doing their own tidying and laundry as soon as they can.

A quick tip for neurodiverse kids, or adults, with executive dysfunction is teaching them to set their own alarms for basic daily tasks.

As they get older you can fold in other life skills. Map use, making their own doctor appointments, or mailing a letter. The list is endless, but it starts with home chores.

CHAPTER 9
Deschooling

Okay! That was a lot of topics! If you've made it this far, I'll assume you are seriously considering letting your child choose their own learning. This means we need to briefly discuss Deschooling.

Remember back when you went to school. Was it fun? Demanding? Exciting? Intense? Easy? Whatever your feelings were, your kids are probably way more stressed than you were. With greater pressure on schools these days to teach science and math, it starts younger each year.

I remember learning the alphabet and what numbers were in kindergarten. Instead, my five year old daughters were learning subtraction and how to read. My oldest began pre-algebra in fourth grade. A year later, my younger daughter learned the same information in third grade.

Both of them were pressured to read faster. Faster, faster, faster. They had timed reading tests each week to make sure they were reading on track. When they failed to meet any expectations, I was reprimanded at parent-teacher conferences. The strain these kids are under is enormous. They are beginning to crack. Burnout and depression being diagnosed as young as eight years old.

My eleven-year-old was talking wistfully about suicide. Therapy didn't help. What finally fixed things was removing the stress. Removing them from school.

Registering them as homeschooled freed them. Not free from learning, but from stressful learning.

The first week they were at home, I was in hyper-mom-mode. Saying, "Let's do some science!" or "Let's go to the library and pick some books!" I truly didn't understand why they were wandering around the house like zombies. They were free, right? Time to live it up!

For the first week of unschooling, my daughters did nothing but play video games and watch online videos. I eventually realized they were recovering. The source of the stress was gone, but the exhaustion would take a while to fade.

I could relate. There were a couple of jobs I'd had that even after finding better work, the specter of them hung over me. I'd find myself going into a job I actually liked, with the worrying feelings from my past job. Waiting for the other shoe to drop or for someone to yell at me. After leaving one particularly stressful work environment, the worst ever, I didn't feel normal for over six months.

In joining some unschooling communities, I found a name for this trauma recovery after leaving the classroom. Deschooling. It made sense, but I thought a few weeks would be enough, so after about three weeks, I announced, "Deschooling is over! Learn something!"

My youngest jumped into it, but my oldest only did a bit of math, then a couple of days later had completely returned to only video games and videos. I didn't say anything, and another month went by, so I made another announcement, "Deschooling is over! Learn something!" Again there were a couple of days of forced learning. My daughter was forcing herself into it for my benefit, but I could tell it was bringing back some of the old anxieties. So, we went back to video games and videos.

I realized Deschooling would take much longer than I thought for my oldest, and I started internally panicking about how long and if she would ever learn anything. Two full months in, she asked for a microphone to practice starting her own channel. When it arrived, she eagerly spent an afternoon drawing art to scan in for her video. When the art was ready, she learned a new video editing software and created her first video all in one day!

It turned out she had been watching animators the whole time and getting ideas for her own art. Not only was she creating again, but in her good mood about art, she returned to her chatty self that night and surprised me with some facts over dinner about healthy eating and black holes. Apparently, she'd also been learning more than art in the videos.

If you presented this to an educator, an afternoon of art and a few science facts, they would probably not call it good progress for two month's worth of learning. However, I was overjoyed at seeing my daughter happy for the first time in years. I took it as a good sign. A step toward fragile regrowth of her love of learning.

Before you can start unschooling, or even regular homeschooling, there should be a break. Like a fallow field. True, a field with no crops is unproductive. However, it's resting and rejuvenating. So, when crops are planted later, the soil can handle it. Deschooling is exactly the same.

One mom put it best in a single sentence. I'm paraphrasing, but it was something along the lines of, "If your child had broken legs, would you tell them to jump up and run?" If you've found this book, it's probably because your child has been damaged by the school system, and they need time for those wounds to heal.

So, plan to leave time for rest after pulling them out of school. Take a few weeks, even a month. Maybe even two months. Then, ease into things. Let them pick their favorite topic first, and reassure them they only need to focus on that one thing for now. Deeper learning will proceed later, and in the meantime, healing will happen.

CHAPTER 10
Laws & GED

Transcripts

A question asked a lot by beginners on the homeschool boards is multiple versions of, "What do I tell people?" or the variation, "What do I tell the state?" The thought of getting in trouble with the law, or their in-laws, is at the forefront of most parent's minds when considering moving toward homeschooling, much less unschooling.

For my own peace of mind, we tried tracking and then moved to transcripts. Some of these things are necessary, depending on which state you live in. Examples of both can be found at the online shop of the publisher of this book. The link is in the resources section at the end. Although you don't need to use exactly what I used, create what feels comfortable for your family.

Tracking could be quite in-depth or really basic. In the beginning, after Deschooling was finished, it was a good way to gauge how involved my kids were in trying out new things. They used a form I created based on state curriculum requirements and other interesting topics. The form eventually became the structure of this book. I called it: Learning for the Week. Basically, both a tracking sheet and a reminder of all the fun ways and things to learn.

By the end of the week, the girls marked the heck out of their pages. It was a fun look at what they chose to do each week. Also, I could ask them about what they learned, and the tracking was a helpful reminder. It kept me involved and let me suggest resources they may not have known about.

Once we hit a rhythm about a year in, they stopped using the form. At first, I tried to force them back into tracking, but eventually, I decided it was not important long term because no one would go back through these daily worksheets anyway. So, we switched to transcripts.

Transcripts are just like they sound. A list of "classes" taken, along with the year and grade level. Whatever interests my daughter was pursuing that year, we turned into classes. Some examples are: How Food Works, History of Astronomy, History of Crime, and Science of Psychology. If your kids need transcripts in the future, a notarized copy of these courses organized by year could be lengthy and impressive.

As I understand it, many states actually require tracked transcripts, so carefully learn exactly what your state requires and follow their rules. Even if you must create your own course names as we do.

I have heard other states don't require a transcript, but instead have forms for filling out your curriculum plan. Apparently, it's best to leave descriptions vague for those. Simply say you are homeschooling and you plan to teach traditional subjects like reading, math, and English.

In the long view of history, formal school is a relatively new ideal, and laws about school are even newer. Fulfill what you must for the state, then embrace more flexible methods of learning.

Testing

When that principal told my mom the school system was broken, the thing stuck in her head was a comment from him, "We do more crowd control at schools than learning. What we teach these kids in a full school day, they can learn at home in less than an hour." It's more true today in an age of instant information than it was when he said it back in the early 90s.

The principal also told her they don't have enough teacher time for each student, adding, "Most kids graduate at an eighth-grade reading level. We are not able to do enough for the kids. They are better off at home."

I only remember these concepts because my mom often quoted him. However, from watching my girls, it feels correct because everything was about crowd control and keeping the kids on the same track.

In school, they were only allowed to read books with their "reading level" dot on them. They could technically read other books, but only the dot-level books from the school library counted for their homework, so that's what they read.

Also, they were only allowed to read one chapter per week for their classroom book club reads, so it took weeks to get to the end of a book. My kids left school in the 4th and 6th grades. My 4th grader was reading at a 5th-grade level, and my 6th grader was reading at a 3rd-grade level.

After only a year and a half of unschooling, their reading ability both soared into adult levels. Everything helped. Being allowed to read any interesting website, communicating with family through messenger, chatting with gaming friends, and using captions on youtube videos. Without being test timed, the girls could read what they found exciting and do it slow enough to appreciate it.

Depending on the state you live in, testing might be required at various ages to make sure your children are on track with their reading and learning. In Oregon, testing happens for the 5th, 8th, and 10th grades. The consequences of failing are only that the child must try the test later.

When my youngest daughter did the 5th-grade test, her results came back at a 5th-grade level, except for reading. Her reading was already at a 12th-grade level. I remember doing the same in Arizona for my 5th-grade homeschool test. I hit all the levels they wanted from me plus more, and my reading level was high in both that test and later in my GED test.

Less than half the states even require testing. From those, only a handful have a penalty worse than simply retaking the test after a bit more study. So, don't worry about the state testing.

In fact, reassure your kids too. Tell them not to worry about it either. Your kids will pass or they will fail. Either way, you'll know they have more in their head than the history of helmets. If they fail, take a moment to study a little next time, state tests always have study guides.

GED

GED is a test you take at the end of homeschooling when you're all done. The test is a little intimidating because it takes a full day to complete. Although, one full day of testing is better than wasting four long years in high school.

When I did it in the 90s, it was an in-person five-subject test with a physical paperback study guide the size and thickness of a cereal box. If you failed, you weren't allowed to try again for months.

These days everything you need to know for the online four-subject test is in the online study guides linked to explanation videos. Better, they have your child take a practice test before the real one to decide if they are ready.

Signing up for training classes through the GED website gives your child access to learning resources for 90 days. Which implies it only takes about three months to prepare for the GED. If you're prepared, the GED is completely doable.

One worry most parents have, is that a high school equivalency diploma will be looked down upon in the future. However, I've had no problem with mine, and neither has my brother. In fact, no one has cared at all. Not colleges and universities we've attended. Not jobs we've held. These days it's even more common to see, now that homeschooling is a bit more mainstream than it was back in the day. When filling out job applications, or building a resume, simply put "Homeschooled GED" in the field for the name of the high school.

Reassure your child that passing is passing and the score doesn't matter. Also remind them they can always retake the test. So, keep things light, take the pressure off, remind them not to stress, and always look at the big picture.

Note, it's simple to get a GED at age 18, but possible to get one at 16 depending on your state's laws. Getting the GED at 16 lets your child begin their career prep much earlier by taking basic courses at a community college the term after the results are official.

The
Resources

Start by thinking of every subject as an elective. Why is calculus more important than painting? It's not, really. It's where you choose to put your focus that matters. In art, there is a concept that if you try to do everything, you can never master anything. The same is true of learning.

Imagine splitting up your day into hour increments, and no matter what you are working on when the clock strikes the hour, you must drop everything you are doing and shift to something completely different. Time-keeping by subject is what our schools are torturing children with. So, provide these resources to your child a little at a time, and if they like one enough to spend all day on it, great!

Becoming fascinated by a subject is a human trait, and especially a neurodiverse trait. So, by knowing how and where to find resources to learn more, your child will never stop learning.

Books

The remarkable people I summarized at the end of chapter one for homeschooling examples were inspired by the book *"Legendary Learning: The Famous Homeschoolers' Guide to Self-Directed Excellence" by Jamie McMillin*. Reading that book is what helped everything click together for me when researching homeschooling for my kids. My favorite point in the book, and something I touched on in this book, is that the government doesn't mandate a curriculum for every age of humans. Only those ages 5 through 18, which is odd and arbitrary. People, including kids and teenagers, should be allowed to learn what interests them, which is the basis of unschooling.

The bit about the vicars in chapter two was inspired by the book *"At Home: A Short History of Private Life" by Bill Bryson*. I highly recommend anything by Bill Bryson, a shining example of someone who learns just by leaving his house. Or, in this specific book's case, by not leaving his house.

"Kids Summer Academy" workbooks by ArgoPrep are great if your child is worried about not being on the same level as kids their age. It's meant to give kids a "review" of what they learned in school that year. So, I provided these workbooks to my kids to show them what they were missing in the grade, and it let them feel caught up in their grade without stressing them out.

The easiest instrument to have on hand is a keyboard piano. You can usually get a used one locally. I've often found both girls, together or separate, playing around on the keyboard. The absolute best book for beginners is *"Teaching Little Fingers to Play: A Book for the Earliest Beginner" by John Thompson*.

Finally, starting to think ahead, another recommended book with unconventional ideas is *"Not Under My Roof: Parents, Teens, and the Culture of Sex" by Amy T. Schalet.*

Games

These are the online games mentioned...

Word of Jumpstart:
www.jumpstart.com/world-of-jumpstart

Roblox:
www.roblox.com

Minecraft Online Community:
www.minecraft.net/en-us

Online Learning Videos and Lessons

Most of my girl's learning took place online. They each had a Chromebook similar to what they were used to at school. I taught them how to bookmark links in their browser, so they always knew how to get their favorite sites.

Options my girls loved and used often:

Khan Academy - Free Lessons by Grade: www.khanacademy.org

DuoLingo - Free Foreign Language Lessons: www.duolingo.com

Dreambox - Subscription to Math Lessons: www.dreambox.com

IXL - Subscription to Lessons by Grade Level: www.ixl.com

Outschool - Paid Lessons: www.outschool.com

Jam - Paid Art Lessons: www.Jam.com

SkillShare - Subscription for Lessons:
www.skillshare.com

Udemy - Paid Lessons:
www.udemy.com

Kiwi Co - Subscription to Monthly Mailed Kits:
www.kiwico.com

Center Stage Ukulele - Paid Online Lessons:
www.csukuleleacademy.com

Other options they tried out:

Class Central - Free and Paid Lessons:
www.class-central.com/subjects

Craftsy! - Free AND Paid Art lessons:
www.craftsy.com/a/shop/free-online-classes

Creative Live - Paid Lessons:
www.creativelive.com

Coursera - Paid Lessons:
www.coursera.org

Master Class - Subscription for Online Lessons:
www.masterclass.com

Great Courses - Subscription for Lessons:
www.thegreatcoursesplus.com

Sparketh - Subscription to Art Lessons:
www.sparketh.com

One Year Novel - Subscription for Writing:
www.clearwaterpress.com/oneyearnovel/

Gentle Guitar - Paid Online Lessons:
www.gentleguitar.com

Hoffman Academy - Free and Paid Lessons:
www.hoffmanacademy.com

Home School Piano - Paid Piano Lessons:
www.homeschoolpiano.com

Printables

Publisher's site for finding materials related to this book, including editable transcripts and printable tracking pages.

www.etsy.com/shop/EarthyInfo

Examples:

High School Homeschool Transcripts

Student Name	Student Social	Institution	
NAME	000-00-0000	Homeschool in Austin, Texas	
Ongoing GPA	Final GPA	Graduation Date	
TBD	TBD	TBD	

9th Grade – 2020/2021 – Cumulative GPA:			
MATHEMATICS	Quarter Term	Date Completed	Grade
Middle School Math Review	SEASON YEAR	00/00 – 00/00	-
Life Skills Math	SEASON YEAR	00/00 – 00/00	A
Pre-Algebra Concepts Overview	SEASON YEAR	00/00 – 00/00	A
LANGUAGE (reading, spelling, grammar)	Quarter Term	Date Completed	Grade
English Grammar	SEASON YEAR	00/00 – 00/00	A
How Memory Works	SEASON YEAR	00/00 – 00/00	A
How Food Works	SEASON YEAR	00/00 – 00/00	A
HISTORY and GOOD CITIZENSHIP (*see volunteer work)	Quarter Term	Date Completed	Grade
Health & PE	SEASON YEAR	00/00 – 00/00	A
History of Crime	SEASON YEAR	00/00 – 00/00	A
U.S. History 101	SEASON YEAR	00/00 – 00/00	A
SCIENCE	Quarter Term	Date Completed	Grade
History of Astronomy	SEASON YEAR	00/00 – 00/00	A
Science of Psychology	SEASON YEAR	00/00 – 00/00	A
Microbiology Basics	SEASON YEAR	00/00 – 00/00	A

10th Grade – 2021/2022 – Cumulative GPA:

11th Grade – 2022/2023 – Cumulative GPA:

12th Grade – 2023/2024 – Cumulative GPA:

DATE RANGE	VOLUNTEER WORK

Parent/Guardian in Charge of Homeschooling	Notary	Notary Stamp
Print _____	Print _____	
Sign _____	Sign _____	
Date_____	Date_____	

Weekly Learning, for _____

Each cube is 15 minutes, mark and circle what you complete, this sheet is for the DATES OF ___/___/___ to ___/___/___

LEARNING

Art □□□□□□□□ □□
--Learning Options: learning videos, making art, reading books about historical art, taking classes
--Topics: Animation, Ceramics, Charcoal, Digital Drawing, Drawing, Felting, Film (making videos), Floral Design,
Food(culinary art), Literature (writing), Painting, Performing (acting), Photography, Sculpture, Sewing, Watercolor

History □□□□□□□□ □□□
--Learning Options: learning videos, reading books, taking classes
--Topics: American History, Famous People, Rights Movements, Wars and Conflicts
History by... Continent, Country, Region, Era/Age, Period & *History of...* Art, Culture, Religion, Science, Technology

Languages □□□
--Learning Options: learning websites, Duolingo, learngaelic.net, learning videos, classes, practice with a partner
--Topics: French, German, Italian, Irish Gaelic, Japanese, Scottish Gaelic, Sign Language, Spanish, Welsh

Math □□□□ □□□
--Learning Options: Khan Academy, Dreambox, learning Website
--Topics: learn by grade level, or what is interesting to you

Music □□□□□□□□□□ □□□
--Learning Options: learning videos, taking classes, practicing what you've learned
--Topics: learning an instrument (guitar, piano, ukulele, violin), music history, playing music, writing music

PE and Outdoors □□□□□□□□□□ □□□
--Learning Options: aquatics center, in the neighborhood, in nature, rec center, workout DVDs
--Topics: Dancing, Hiking, Nature Walk, Roller Skating or Blading, Scootering, Swimming, Walking, Zumba

Science □□□□□□□□□□ □□□
--Learning Options: learning videos, reading books, taking classes
--Topics: Anatomy, Astronomy, Biology, Botany, Chemistry, Climatology, Earth science, Environmental studies, First Aid,
Geology, Health studies, Marine studies, Nutrition, Oceanography, Physics, Science History, Zoology

Social Studies □□□□□□ □□□
--Learning Options: learning videos, reading books, taking classes
--Topics: Anthropology, Archaeology, Current Events And News, Economics, Geography, Global News, History, Human
Behavior, Laws, Legends and Mythology, Philosophy, Political Science, Psychology, Religion, Sociology

Reading Fiction □□□□□□□□□□□□□□□□ □□
--Learning Options: physical book, audio book
--Topics: Comedy, Fantasy, Mythology, Adventure, Mystery, Science fiction, Drama, Romance, Horror

Reading Nonfiction □□□□□□□□□□ □□□
--Learning Options: reliable website, physical book, magazine, audio book, audio book video
--Topics: *Can be double counted with... History, Science, Social Studies*

Writing □□□□□□□□□□ □□□
--Learning Options: writing about a topic, about a book, a fiction story, for a slide show, or typing practice
--Topics: *Can be double counted with... History, Science, Social Studies*

LIVING

Social □□□
Time with: Pet, Friend, Sister, Dad, Mom, Aunt, Uncle, Grandma, or Amino

Tidying □□□
Tidy Bedroom, Dishes, Counters, Front Room/Entry, Bathroom, Laundry, Vacuum, Sweep, Pets: Feed/Water/Litterbox

Playing □□□
Card Games, Board Games, Video Games, Movies, Shows, Online Videos, Puzzles

Volunteering

This is a great way to get your teen homeschooler out and about. Plus it looks good on a resume!

I volunteered at a nearby hospital at age 14, and because of my stellar volunteering record I was able to get a job there at 16 after my GED results came through. I continued to volunteer until age 19 because I loved the hospital and people so much.

I also volunteered with my library's YAAC group, writing reviews for pre-released books provided by the publisher and writing reviews for the library's teen newsletter. The experience I gained at both of these unpaid jobs was invaluable.

My daughters have also volunteered and it really makes a difference in how they think about the world and the types of jobs they can get in the future. Volunteer and intern experience is just as valid as paid work on a resume. Also, it helps with college applications, some of which require some kind of volunteer experience.

Most places want volunteers at least 14 and older, but occasionally you can find options as young as twelve. Also, if you know anyone running their own business, your child can intern for your friends and gain valuable experience that way too!

Encourage your kids to volunteer as much as

possible in at least three places. Research these options starting around age 12. Make a plan of which places they are interested in for what ages to be sure to apply on time. Sometimes orientation only happens once or twice a year and you don't want to miss those dates.

Searching your city + "internships for high school students" or "youth volunteers" are places to start. Also trying "remote youth internship" or "remote youth volunteer" and "virtual youth volunteer" might bring up something your child is excited about. More great places to look for unpaid work are local non-for-profits like animal shelters, hospitals, or libraries.

Your state + Humane Society should bring up an address to your closest shelter.

Check all your local hospitals for positions called "Junior Volunteer" or "Youth Volunteer", (the past name was Candy Striper).

Also check nearby libraries for titles like "Library Youth Volunteer" or "Teen Volunteer" or YAAC.

Some research to see if your city has a local chapter of the Youth Volunteer Corps is not always easy, check with your local community center to ask about Youth Volunteer Corps or if they know of any other volunteer options.

Finally, looking for a local chapter of your boy scouts or girl scouts is another way to get a child involved in the local community and get some volunteer experience.

In the same vein of a youth organization is finding a local 4H club (4-h.org).

Both scouting and 4H can also be put on a resume and college application along with volunteering and internships.

The
Conclusion

Humans retain learning when they are engaged in the topic, and children are not any different. Forced subjects on a schedule may help some children thrive, but with increased awareness of neurodiversity, it's also ever more obvious how the current system is not supporting creative learning. All kids could benefit from being allowed to learn in a way that suits them best, but especially creative thinkers. From restricted interests to hyper-focus, kids who don't fit into the school mold must have options for an independent approach to education.

A diet is a short-term method of eating with a specific outcome in mind, while healthy eating is a lifestyle change. Similarly, a college degree is a short-term learning method with a specific outcome in mind, while unschooling is a lifestyle change. Leave the strict college-style learning to later, because college will be easier if they've spent their life learning to love learning.

BIO

Starr Green is an autistic creative thinker and raised two happy kids. She lives in Corvallis Oregon and has a degree specializing in Environmental Communication from Oregon State University. Find out more at: starrgreeninfo.com

Printed in Great Britain
by Amazon

27838704R00047